Walking On Water

Finding Peace In The Storms Of Life

Gary Byford

ECCLESIA PUBLISHING

Dedication photo by Kim Byford of the Sea of Galilee 2010.

All Scripture, unless otherwise specified are taken from the New King James Version®. Copyright © 1982 by Thomas Nelson. Used by permission. All rights reserved.

ISBN: 978-1-7772784-7-2

Edited, Produced, Published by Ecclesia Publishing
Cover Design by Ecclesia Publishing
ecclesiapublishing@gmail.com
www.ecclesiapublishing.com

Dedication

To my dear wife Kim who has passed through the storm and now waits on the other side.

Photo of the Sea of Galilee, Israel taken by Kim Byford – November 2010

TABLE OF CONTENTS

FOREWORD

In 2010 our family saw several significant changes to our lives beginning in May with my wife's mother coming to live with us. She had lived on her own for fifteen years after my father-in-law died. After a checkup at the hospital, following a minor accident at home, the doctor told my wife and her brother that their mother couldn't live on her own anymore and would need to stay with one of them. Kim called me that night and asked if she could stay with us. I said that was fine, and we prepared the living room on the first floor since she could no longer climb stairs.

The next change was in June when we started attending another church after leaving the one we were previously at for about eight years. Kim had finally gotten her ministerial diploma after seven years of night courses and she was looking forward to serving at a ministerial level at the church we were at presently. However, there was not an opening for her at that time.

After being invited by one of our friends to a new church they had started to attend, Kim felt at home and saw the chance to be used by the Lord there. We started attending regularly and agreed as a family to make this our new church home.

At the end of August, while my daughter and her husband were on vacation, I had the use of their car. As I drove their car to church one Sunday with the family and a friend, I accidentally went through a red light. Immediately, we were T-boned by a car coming through on the driver's side of the vehicle, pushing our car to the curb. Thankfully, the other driver was not hurt, but my wife and our friend sustained relatively minor injuries and were taken to the hospital to be checked out and treated. My son and I were fortunate and had almost no injuries, so we stayed at the scene while I filled out the police report and waited for the tow truck to arrive. The kid's car was totaled in the accident, so I offered to pay for its replacement.

I later went to the hospital to see my wife and friend to find out how they were doing. Although they were shaken up and had some bruising, they were released to come home that same day.

Around the middle of September, just a couple of weeks later, we were able to move into a disability-adapted home within our community which was much more convenient for my mother-in-law. Of the three bedrooms, one was on the main floor and was attached to her own washroom with amenities that were more suited to her needs.

Lastly, at the end of September, I was laid off from my job of thirty-two years as a competitor had bought our company. Since I was working for a large multinational company, I was given over a year and a half between the announcement and my last day. During that time, they informed us about our severance packages and outlined the various benefits and agencies the company would pay for, which would help me in my search for new employment.

Since I knew the date of my departure, I tried holding on to as much of my vacation time as possible throughout the year so it could be added to my package when I left. However, given all of the other events we encountered that year, this left me totally exhausted. I said that I wasn't going to look for a new job until January of the following year to rest and take time to focus on our home after the move and deal with the fallout from the car accident.

With the number of years I had worked at my previous employer, the package I received was generous and was meant to last for quite a while should it take longer than expected to find a new job. This was wonderful as the timing would help with many of the events I already described.

When we were in the planning stage of our move, I told Kim that this was a rare opportunity to update much of our furniture, some of which were still original when we got married over thirty years ago. I said we could have the new furniture delivered to our new address, so we don't have to move it and have the old furniture taken away.

Kim also fulfilled one of her dreams by going on a tour of Israel with one of the ministries we enjoyed on television. I declined to go because it was way too expensive for both of us. In the end though, I'm not sure which was more expensive, the trip or the things she brought back!

Within a few months into the new year, it was evident that the finances that were meant to sustain us much longer were slowly drying up, and I didn't have any prospects for a new job at that point. I started watching our budget much closer, but by June of 2011, our finances were all gone as if it had evaporated with the onset of the warm summer weather!

To make it to the end of the month, I eventually had to approach my daughter and son-in-law and asked to borrow the equivalent of half a month's expenses just to get to the end of June. If I didn't find work by then, I had no other resources I could rely on to go further. What started off so bright and promising now ended due to faulty assumptions of how fast I would be rehired.

In these situations, the problem quickly becomes an obsession that dominated my thoughts and focus. Doubts started to creep in, such as, *"what will we do if we can't pay our rent for July? How will we be able to afford groceries? Will we need to think about moving in with our kids?"*

One morning, in the midst of all this, I woke up and lay in bed for a bit. While I lay there, I sensed the Lord say to me, *"get out of the boat."* Now I know many other Christians have an ongoing dialogue where they hear the voice of God speaking and directing them on a regular basis, but I didn't. I lay there wondering what God was telling me. I was sure He wasn't just telling me to get out of bed. So I asked the Lord, *"what do you mean: Get out of the boat?"* The Lord replied that He wanted me to write about it, and as I write, I would understand the meaning.

The Lord knew my passion for writing and chose to use it to lead me through the scriptures to a place where He would confront me with the obstacle that was standing between myself and the answer to my prayers.

When I thought of the words *"Get out of the boat,"* the only image that came to mind was that of Peter getting out of the boat to walk to Jesus on the water in the midst of the storm out on the lake. This was one of my favorite stories in the New Testament, but I couldn't see what this had to do with my lack of money and quest for work. So I decided to reread the story and turn my heart toward digging deeper to find just what God was trying to tell me.

I hope to share some of the incredible truths and principles I discovered within this passage in the pages that follow. They have changed my life by helping me see God differently. That shift in how I saw God has impacted my faith and my confidence in Him to meet all of my needs and remind me that He is always with me no matter what storm I may be in.

PREFACE

When Adam and Eve ate the forbidden fruit in the Garden of Eden, the presence of God was lifted from mankind along with their innocence. The intimacy they enjoyed with their Creator had left as God could no longer remain with them now that sin had entered in. At that moment, both God and man suffered the loss for which man was created — relationship.

Our God is a relational God who created us for the purpose of living with Him in a bond of love and fellowship as His children. He is our Heavenly Father, and we were made in His image. However, the family is now separated, and closeness has given way to distance. Speaking to our Father no longer takes place in the cool of the day but through the avenue of prayer.

Prayer is our lifeline and our seamless place of communication with God. As our lungs cannot do without the unconscious practice of breathing in and out the life-giving air around us, we should be in constant prayer throughout each day, breathing out our thoughts and requests to the Lord and breathing in the voice of God as we listen for His responses. Paul reminds us in scripture to *"pray without ceasing"* ~ 1 Thessalonians 5:17.

We only have to look at Jesus to see how important prayer was in both His life and ministry while He was on this earth. He would slip away to be with His Father, spending hours, often alone at night, in prayer. His relationship with His Father was always His priority, and fulfilling the Father's will was His singular focus and purpose for which He left Heaven.

This now becomes the model for our spiritual life and growth. Our relationship with God and the fulfillment of His plan for our life should be our priority. This foundation will help us to weather the storms that come our way and enable us to arrive at the destination God has set out for us.

We maintain our spiritual health now in similar ways to our physical health. We dine daily on spiritual bread by reading God's Word so that it transforms us by renewing our minds and changing us more and more into the image of Jesus. Jesus said that *"Man shall not live by bread alone, but by every word that proceeds from the mouth of God"* ~ Matthew 4:4.

Finding Peace In The Storms Of Life

Immediately Jesus made His disciples get into the boat and go before Him to the other side while He sent the multitudes away. And when He had sent the multitudes away, He went up on the mountain by Himself to pray. Now when evening came, He was alone there. But the boat was now in the middle of the sea, tossed by the waves, for the wind was contrary.

Now in the fourth watch of the night, Jesus went to them, walking on the sea. And when the disciples saw Him walking on the sea, they were troubled, saying, "It is a ghost!" And they cried out for fear. But immediately, Jesus spoke to them, saying, "Be of good cheer! It is I; do not be afraid."

And Peter answered Him and said, "Lord, if it is You, command me to come to You on the water."

So He said, "Come." And when Peter had come down out of the boat, he walked on the water to go to Jesus. But when he saw that the wind was boisterous, he was afraid; and beginning to sink, he cried out, saying, "Lord, save me!"

And immediately Jesus stretched out His hand and caught him, and said to him, "O you of little faith, why did you doubt?" And when they got into the boat; the wind ceased. Then those who were in the boat came and worshiped Him, saying, "Truly You are the Son of God."

Peter had the courage to do what none of the other disciples thought was possible. What Jesus said to Peter, He now says to all of us, *"do not be afraid, it is I. Come."* It's at that moment that we realize. We really were made for walking on water. ~ Matthew 14: 22-33.

Chapter 1

THE CALM BEFORE

"And when Jesus went out, He saw a great multitude; and He was moved with compassion for them, and healed their sick." Matthew ~ 14:14

Sometimes in life, there are days that feel like we're on a rollercoaster of ups and downs, filled with events, experiences, and emotions that are driving us, and we're simply swept along for the ride. Jesus and His disciples were having one of those days. It started with news of the beheading of Jesus' cousin, John the Baptist. When Jesus heard what had happened to John, He withdrew by boat to a solitary place.

John's death must have been especially painful for Jesus as their lives were intertwined before they were born to the day of Jesus' baptism. John was busy preparing the way for Jesus by baptizing those who came out to see him, preaching that the Kingdom of God is near and for them to repent of their sins and be baptized. He was the one who announced Jesus as He was coming to him to be also baptized as *"the Lamb of God who takes away the sins of the world."* This proclamation and subsequent baptism would mark the start of Jesus' public ministry.

However, when the crowds heard where Jesus had gone, they followed on foot from the towns to find Him. Although Jesus must have been wearied with grief, He looked out and saw the crowds and had compassion on them and healed the sick among them.

As it was now getting late in the day and they were out in a remote place, the disciples wanted to send the crowd to buy food in the villages. But Jesus wanted to teach the disciples a lesson about God's provision and unlimited resources. He catches them off guard by telling them that the people don't need to leave but for them to give the crowd something to eat.

I'm sure that the disciples must have been completely befuddled as to what Jesus was expecting them to do. They were used to seeing Jesus perform miracles, except now He was telling them to do the impossible. This would be another teaching opportunity that Jesus would use to show how God's resources have no limits.

The disciples told Jesus that there were only five loaves and two fish. Undeterred by their doubts, Jesus asked them to bring the food to Him and commanded the crowd to sit down on the grass. Then taking the bread and fish in His hands, He blessed them and gave out the portions to the disciples to distribute to the multitude. To the amazement of everyone, the food kept on coming. Jesus continued to break the bread and fish until all had been fed and filled. In the end, they took up twelve baskets of fragments left over, and the scriptures record that there were five thousand men, not including women and children, who partook of this miracle.

Jesus did not just stand there and call down manna from Heaven to feed the crowd; instead, He chose to partner with us by asking us to share what we have with Him. Then when we are willing to let go and place our possessions in Jesus' hands, He, in turn, releases the power of God to multiply our resources to meet whatever the need is from the Father's unlimited storehouse.

At that point, John, in his gospel, says that Jesus perceived that the crowd was preparing to take Him by force to make Him king. Therefore, Jesus quickly sends His disciples off in a boat to go before Him to the other side of the lake while He sent the crowds away. After that, scripture tells us, *"He when up on the mountain by Himself to pray."*

Jesus had no interest in becoming an earthly king, being moved around and used by the crowds to lead them in their quest to overcome the power of Rome over their lives. He would not give in to that temptation any more than when the devil tried to tempt Him in the wilderness by offering Him all the kingdoms of the world if He would bow down and worship him. Jesus was steadfast and could not be distracted from His true purpose of fulfilling the will of His Father.

The disciples, for their part, had just experienced a mountaintop miracle of feeding thousands as Jesus multiplied the food for them to give out. At this point, it's good to remember that after we come down from our mountain top experiences, we will often be confronted with an equally difficult situation that tests and can often sap the joy we had just felt. Such would be the case as the disciples headed out to cross the lake.

For us, it's important to know that there will always be distractions and temptations which will try to divert us from our course, especially after our mountain top experiences, to get us to leave the path the Lord has been leading us on. However, when we allow that to happen, we will usually end up finding we're going down a dead-end road. At times like this, we quickly need to repent and get back on the path that God has laid out for us to find true success and fulfillment.

Jesus didn't allow temptations to distract Him. His focus was on spending time in prayer. Prayer for Jesus is much like air is to us. His desire to spend time alone in communion with His Father was precious and essential in His mission to fulfill the role the Father had given Him.

Storm Proofs

- Heaven's resources have no limits.
- Do not allow distractions to take you off course.

Chapter 2

WHO'S IN CHARGE?

"You are not your own? For you were bought at a price" ~ 1
Corinthians 6:19b-20a

If God was an ocean and you were merely standing on the shore looking out, how far are you prepared to go? The water seems so vast and deep, and you feel so small and insignificant standing before it. So many questions cross your mind. What's out there? What happens when I cannot touch the bottom? How long can I swim before I can't swim anymore? What will keep me from going under?

In many ways, the imagery of the ocean is like a couple standing at the altar. They are preparing to step out into the future while promising to love and support each other in whatever challenges life may bring. Somehow, those mutual promises seem to establish enough of a foundation for them to let go of any doubts or fears they may have had about the future. The sense of hope and joy they feel as they begin their journey together is drawn from the love and trust they have for each other.

The relationship between Jesus and His Church is often referred to in scripture as a marriage. When we accept Jesus into our lives, we are entering into the new covenant Jesus spoke about at the last supper. While it is a commitment by us to follow Him as Lord and Saviour, it is also a commitment by God that you have become a child of His and heir, along with Jesus, to all that the Father has. The Bible even tells us that our citizenship has now been transferred to Heaven, thus making us ambassadors for Christ while still living on earth.

Like a wedding ceremony, the act of accepting salvation for our sins takes only a few moments, but our lives will never be the same. We don't know what the future holds, yet we are filled with a new sense of peace and excitement at the forgiveness of our past and anticipation of beginning a new life in Christ. This new life shall present situations where we will learn to allow God to become the Lord of our lives.

It is indeed a lifelong process, and Paul encourages us to *"work out your salvation with fear and trembling"* ~ Philippians 2:12b. This refers to our growth in God through our daily submission to His will. Jesus said it this way, *"Then He said to them all, 'If anyone desires to come after Me, let him deny himself, and take up his cross daily, and follow Me.'"* ~ Luke 9:23. Jesus states clearly in this passage that if we are going to follow and live for Him, we will need to deny ourselves and put Him first every day.

The picture of us taking up our cross is a graphic reminder of what it means to deny ourselves. Paul said it another way to illustrate the point in his letter to the Galatians, *"I have been crucified with Christ; it is no longer I who live, but Christ lives in me; and the life which I now live in the flesh I live by faith in the Son of God, who loved me and gave Himself for me."* ~ Galatians 2:20. Paul clearly explains that once we have surrendered our lives to Christ, we must consider ourselves dead to our old nature with its previous will and agenda. We are now alive in Christ by the Holy Spirit living within us.

Following Him now as Lord becomes a conscious act of our will. That's why Jesus tells us that it will be a daily decision. It's not something that runs on autopilot. Our old nature has not gone away, but we do have the choice through the power of the Holy Spirit within us to choose to obey God's commands and follow the leading of His Spirit in the plan He has for our lives.

Giving over the reins of our lives to another may not be something we had to think about before giving our lives to Christ. We all just naturally accepted that we were in complete charge of ourselves. However, in choosing to make Jesus the Lord of our lives, it will do us well to have a daily reminder to turn over the keys of our lives to Him, aka, die daily.

We now take our place in the passenger seat, allowing Jesus to control the direction we are heading. However, many times we can be like the back-seat driver advising on where we think we should be going, shooting our leg out every now and then on invisible brakes when we find ourselves in areas we're not very comfortable visiting.

Over time though, we begin to relax and recognize that God knows exactly what He is doing since He is the One Who is holding our road map. When you spend all your time seated beside someone, you develop a comfort level you didn't have at the beginning because you had no previous experience driving together, especially with someone else at the wheel. Trust starts to build, and it becomes easier to accept the bumps along the way because we know we are heading towards a better destination.

Like the young married couple, the comfort level is equal to the level of intimacy in the relationship where they know each other so well that they feel confident about their future because they are committed to facing everything together - for better or for worse.

The Lord has made the same promise to us. The more we get to know Him, the more we can abide in His peace. When we arrive at that place of peace in our relationship with Him, we are more open to the surrender of our will to His, at a heart level rather than just a head level. It's the same principle as when we first accepted Him into our lives. These are some of the vital steps in our growth to spiritual maturity in Jesus.

All this is to say that if our old self has indeed been crucified and deemed dead, we need to accept that all of our former "rights" concerning our life's direction are also dead. We are now in a covenant relationship with Jesus and the Father, who have the power and authority to direct and protect us and everything we do going forward.

This may sound simple, but the results of this exchange of ownership is far-reaching. First, it requires our total surrender to the Lordship of Jesus, and second, we begin a lifelong journey of discipleship, learning about our Master and how to follow in His footsteps. The closer we draw to Him through our time spent in prayer and the Word, the more intimate the relationship becomes until the ability to withstand the storms of life takes on a new dimension because Jesus is now there with us.

Storm Proofs

- You are covered by God through His covenant as His child and heir.
- As we surrender our will to God we begin a lifelong journey to become like Jesus.
- The Father now cares for and leads us in the path that He has planned just for us.

Chapter 3

THE BLESSING OF ADVERSITY

"As iron sharpens iron, So a man sharpens the countenance of his friend." ~ Proverbs 27:17

When negative things come into our lives, our natural response is to immediately stop, step back and remove ourselves from the path of the threat if possible and any impact it may have upon us. Often, we may go to prayer and ask the Lord to remove the trouble from us, and there are times that this may be the most appropriate thing to do. But what about the times that the problem in front of us doesn't go away?

The truth is, trials are something we will have to deal with until we go to be with the Lord. Job says, *"Yet man is born to trouble, As the sparks fly upward"* ~ Job 5:7. James also tells us:

"My brethren, count it all joy when you fall into various trials, knowing that the testing of your faith produces patience. But let patience have its perfect work, that you may be perfect and complete, lacking nothing." ~ James 1:2-4.

Now I know that trials and joy sound like an oxymoron that doesn't belong in the same sentence. James says we can actually try and look at trials differently and consider them pure joy because of the purpose. He instructs us to be patient by allowing the trials to accomplish its purpose because God is doing a work in us to make us mature and complete.

Adversity or friction is a part of just about every facet of life. From the plots of books and films to the simple reality of juggling the items in our daily schedules because there never seems enough time in the day to do everything. Adversity is something we all face regularly and may show up in the form of stress.

I would often say to my family as they were growing up that we have little to no choice over the things that happen to us, but we do have a choice as to how we will react to them. Those things which I cannot control, I try not to spend much time on, but I am responsible about how I will respond to the matter. Will I react in frustration and anger, or will I let the love of Christ outweigh the issue on the scales of life?

So what are some of the positive aspects of adversity?

Examples In Nature

The natural creation of pearls results from when either a grain of sand or possibly a parasite somehow gets past the edges and comes to rest in either an oyster, mussel, or clam. This is regarded as an irritant that triggers its defenses to produce a liquid called *nacre* to coat the irritant repeatedly until a beautiful pearl is formed. This process may take about three years or more to complete.

The mollusk certainly didn't like the intruder but thought it was a threat and tried to neutralize it. However, the result is a gem that is rare, which was naturally processed by the elements, as opposed to those that are produced with the help of man, but beautiful in either case.

We also see the necessity of adversity or friction when the butterfly is trying to emerge from its cocoon and spread its new wings to fly. However, it's been told that if a well-meaning person were to intervene and pry the cocoon open prematurely so that the butterfly could come out without a struggle, it would never be able to fly. It seems that God designed it so that during the effort the butterfly exerts to free itself from the cocoon, the wings would be strengthened as the blood begin to flow and spread through them. Without that struggle, the butterfly would never realize the purpose of its transformation.

In our spiritual lives, we would all like to grow and mature to the level the Lord is working in us to reach our destiny or purpose and fulfill the plan He has for us. We just don't see adversity as God's tool in shaping and refining us. Adversity, though, is kind of like God's bootcamp with increasing obstacles to push us to limits we would not have attempted on our own. But if we want to soar like an eagle for God, we need to overcome the trials that test us.

It's interesting to note that those we would consider our heroes in the Bible were not immune from adversity. If you examine the lives of just about any of the major characters that come to mind, we could probably call their stories "When Bad Things Happen To God's People." God had them pass through some incredible storms before they emerged on the other side in a place of victory and vindication. We will take a look at some of these stories in another chapter.

God's Gemstones

Before any gemstone is displayed in a store window, miners needed to dig in the earth for the gemstone brought out of the ground in a raw state that would probably not impress any potential customer. However, the gem cutter knows the worth of the stone and begins the process of cleaning, cutting, and polishing the gem until it becomes the image of what he had planned for it. Then it can be put on display for all to enjoy its beauty and worth.

We are God's jewels. Out of compassion for our helpless estate, God sent Jesus down into the darkness of our world to redeem us and bring us out into the light by His marvelous grace. As the Psalmist said in Psalm 40:2, *"He also brought me up out of a horrible pit, out of the miry clay, and set my feet upon a rock, and established my steps."* Only a Saviour could understand the incredible worth that each soul holds in the Father's heart. Therefore, He did what we could not do for ourselves.

When we first stand in God's Kingdom, we are still soiled and dirty from a life of sin. Like any good father, He doesn't just leave us that way but gently sets about cleaning and refining us from the rough condition that we came in. He has a plan and a vision of the person we will become as we yield ourselves into His loving care.

He first washes us in His Son Jesus' purifying blood to remove the toughened layer of dirt-encrusted upon us by sin, which separated us from Him. Once the crust is removed, we get our first glimpse of a stone that is beautiful but still raw. It needs to be shaped and defined by the only One who can give it the purpose it was destined to become.

This is usually an uncomfortable process and most misunderstood as to why we must endure it on our journey of transformation. There are trials and pressures in our new life that we cannot find any meaning in as we pass through them. However, the Master Craftsman works patiently, making the necessary cuts, taking away those things that hold no value, to achieve the form He has chosen.

Finally, as we walk in obedience serving Him faithfully, God is polishing us to shine for Him. We are the creation of His workmanship, precious and living stones on display to the world around us. For He not only saves us but restores us, transforms us, and makes us into something beautiful.

However, the beauty of the gem was only achieved through an intense refining process. I'm sure that if the gem was alive, it would have been totally bewildered and complaining about the purpose of the cutting and polishing it had to endure. Like us, it may only begin to understand the reason when it looks back and sees where it had come from and where it is now.

Storm Proofs

- Adversity is a fact of life, but it is also a tool that God uses to refine us.
- If we want to fly for God, we need to overcome the trials that tests us.
- God will make something beautiful out of our lives if we allow Him to.

Chapter 4

THE STORM

"Now when evening came, He was alone there. But the boat was now in the middle of the sea, tossed by the waves, for the wind was contrary." ~ Matthew 14:23b-24

In obedience to Jesus' instructions, the disciples had gotten into their boat and headed out to the other side of the lake. This command that Jesus had given would not really be a concern to them. They were primarily experienced fishermen who would typically go out at night to fish for a living. This was a task they were familiar with and very much within their comfort zone.

However, conditions had suddenly changed after they left shore, and the weather had now become such that the wind and waves were contrary to them, preventing them from making any headway. They had been able to make it only about three or four miles out, but now it was increasingly apparent that their lives were in danger.

When Jesus came out walking on the water, He wasn't tossed about, stumbling His way amidst the wind and waves. In every situation where the sea threatened to sink the boat, Jesus was either sleeping or calmly stepped into the boat, and the storm died down. He was not bothered by the situation swirling around Him. Jesus had an inner peace that external forces could not shake. It allowed Him to focus on the one thing that consumed Him: *to do the will of His Father.*

It's interesting to note that Jesus didn't continue walking nor did He just get in the boat this time, but He stopped a little way off. When the disciples first saw Him, they are alarmed, thinking it must be a ghost. After all, nobody had seen anyone walk on water before, so what else could it be? Jesus quickly tells them not to be afraid; it was Him!

It is at this point that something very intriguing and marvelous takes place. Of the three Gospels that record this story, Matthew, Mark, and John, only Matthew tells us of Peter's remarkable leap of faith here. Upon hearing Jesus calling out to the disciples not to be afraid, Peter says to Jesus in Matthew 14:28, *"Lord, if it is You, command me to come to You on the water."* Although Peter was known in scripture for acting and speaking impulsively, the question he poses to Jesus demonstrates a boldness of faith that must have left the other disciples asking themselves, *"What did he just say?"*

Then to their further amazement, Jesus responds to Peter by telling him in verse 29, *"Come."* Peter then gets out of the boat and begins to walk to Jesus on the water! With child-like faith, Peter acts upon Jesus' word. They had witnessed so many miracles that Jesus had performed, including feeding the masses who had come to hear Him preach just a few hours earlier with no more to work with than a little boy's lunch. Peter simply believed that if Jesus said it, he could do it.

However, after taking a few steps toward Jesus on the water, Peter becomes distracted. Scripture tells us in verse 30, *"But when he saw that the wind was boisterous, he was afraid; and beginning to sink he cried out, saying, 'Lord, save me!'"* As long as Peter kept his eyes on Jesus, his faith enabled him to do what Jesus had told him. Once Peter's attention left Jesus and began to focus on the circumstances around him, his faith came crashing down like the waves surrounding them, and he began to sink.

Just as Peter walks and sees the wind and waves and starts to sink, it's precisely what the devil would have us do any time we are engaged with God. He tries to distract us and get us to take our eyes off of Jesus and to focus on what we cannot do in our strength. But Jesus empowers to walk on water! Verse 31 states, *"And immediately Jesus stretched out His hand and caught him, and said to him, 'O you of little faith, why did you doubt?'"*

It may seem strange though, that Jesus would chastise Peter for lack of faith. After all, wasn't he the only one of the twelve to get out of the boat and begin to walk to Jesus on the water? I feel that Jesus was speaking to Peter not in disappointment but as encouragement, saying, *"You were doing so well! Why did you stop?"* Matthew then tells us that Peter and Jesus got into the boat, and the wind died down. The love of God is always ready to lift us out of our storms whenever we turn our attention and call upon Him.

As I reflect on this story, I am moved by Peter's faith to be willing to leave the only thing that offered him any sense of safety and protection while stuck in the storm they were in. At that moment, Peter saw more security in the presence of Jesus than the boat he was in.

We are always anxious for God to get in our boat and answer our prayers with what we asked for, though many times, the Lord will ask us to step out of our boat and leave our requests to do things our way. He wants to bring us to a place where we are willing to let go of everything else that we're hanging onto for security and allow Him to have His way. It comes down to a matter of trust.

In our lives, so many of us are content just knowing that Jesus is with us in our boat as we journey through life. He pushed us away from the shore and got in with us when we first invited Him into our hearts. After many years of traveling together, like the disciples, we're in a place we have become used to and know well. The waters are familiar and calm. We feel a sense of control over the situation, and if the weather should change and become a problem, we know we can go to Jesus to calm the waves of our lake so that things can be restored to the way they were once.

But there are times when we are surprised by the sudden changes that can sweep down upon us and catch us off guard. Our boat can be caught up in forces that were neither foreseen nor controllable. The elements on all sides are battering us, and water is slowly seeping in. We immediately look for Jesus, but there seems to be no response when we call out. We try looking for Him, but everything is so dark, and the circumstances make it difficult even to get a sense of where we are or the direction we are headed. This is the situation the disciples found themselves in, but Jesus was not in the boat with them.

Many times, as Christians, we have left ourselves vulnerable to spiritual attacks through simple complacency. We often find ourselves in a place that is relatively peaceful, familiar, and inside of our comfort zone. We feel confident in our abilities to control the circumstances we are in and believe that we can meet any changes to the course we are travelling on.

When things are good, we tend to let down our guard. We shift our focus from looking to God for His direction and protection to relying on our understanding and experience of the situation. Thus we are invariably lulled into a sense of false security. In natural terms, we would say this is the equivalent of "falling asleep at the wheel." Our alert systems and radar are turned off, and we are adrift on the waves of our presumption!

Scripture tells us that *"your adversary the devil walks about like a roaring lion, seeking whom he may devour"* ~ 1 Peter 5:8. We need to be mindful that we are constantly engaged in spiritual warfare against the enemy of our souls. He is always looking for an opening where he can trip us up and get a foothold in the areas of our lives where we are weakest. When things are going well, we tend to rest, leaving ourselves exposed to attacks we didn't see coming and totally unprepared for.

Therefore, when entering into battle, does a soldier wait to dress himself while standing in front of the enemy after the conflict has already begun? The preparation must take place well beforehand, so he is prepared and ready to respond at any given moment.

Paul warns us about spiritual warfare, *"For we do not wrestle against flesh and blood, but against principalities, against powers, against the rulers of the darkness of this age, against spiritual hosts of wickedness in the heavenly places"* ~ Ephesians 6:12. He then lists the various armour and weapons that God has made available to us so that we can stand our ground. It is up to us then to make sure that we are walking in the Spirit and fully clothed in the Lord's armour before we can engage the enemy successfully.

Storm Proofs

- You are never alone - Jesus is always with you.
- God uses storms to challenge our faith and also to step outside of our comfort zone.
- Our relationship with Jesus is our preparedness for the storms.

Chapter 5

WHEN THE ANSWERS DON'T COME

"A man's steps are of the LORD; How then can a man understand his own way?" ~ Proverbs 20:24

How do you react when something you have fervently prayed about seemingly goes unanswered? Unanswered prayer is an area that every Christian has to come to terms with from time to time. I must admit that this was an issue that had caused me a lot of frustration and misunderstanding when I was a younger Christian. In general, I was not a very patient person at that time, and this is still something that the Lord is working on in me even now.

We live in an instant society, and as part of that "instant society," when I was waiting for an answer to something, such as a reply to an email, a follow-up phone call, etc., it wouldn't be long before I would either be on the phone tracking them down or in their doorway—if it was at work—to get the answer I was looking for.

When we do not receive the answer we had prayed for, we can come to many wrong conclusions as to why. We may think that it wasn't important enough to God or that we were not in a place of right standing with Him before we prayed. However, many times it can be just a matter of God having a different outcome in His plan that could never happen if He did as we asked. Over the years, this had matured in my life where I've learned to accept when my prayers did not get answered the way I wanted them. I trust that the Lord is saying, *"I've got something better."* At that point, I try to leave it with Him and trust the direction He is leading.

Many times, when my wife and I had prayed about situations, asking God to intervene, sometimes things didn't work out the way we hoped. It appeared that the Lord was leading in a different direction, and we trusted Him to take care of it.

In those times when our lives seem under attack, we need to remember that we belong to the Lord, and He will fight for us so that we can be strengthened. Even if we may not understand and have no control of the situation or its consequences, we know that He never leaves us nor forsakes us.

In the Old Testament, Elisha had a situation where the King of Syria was coming to capture him because he was warning the King of Israel of the King of Syria's attempts to attack Israel as they were at war. The king was so frustrated that he sent horses and chariots and a great army to surround the city in the middle of the night to capture Elisha.

Now when the servant of Elisha got up the following day and went out and saw the army surrounding the city, he went back and asked Elisha, "alas, my master! What shall we do?" So he answered, "Do not fear, for those who are with us are more than those who are with them." And Elisha prayed and said, "LORD, I pray, open his eyes that he may see." Then the LORD opened the eyes of the young man, and he saw. And behold, the mountain was full of horses and chariots of fire all around Elisha ~ 2 Kings 6: 15b-17.

Besides the storms we can see, I believe that there are many times that the Lord has protected us from attacks from the spiritual world that we were not even aware of. Like Elisha, the Lord fights on our behalf in ways that are not always evident to us. As our Heavenly Father, He stands between us and any harm that may touch His children. Those times that we do encounter trials are opportunities to grow in faith and perseverance.

The life of a Christian is a life of surrender. I need to surrender my right to know or understand every point along the path of God's plan for me before I will submit to His Will. A refusal to submit is evidence that He is no longer the Lord of my life. I have taken back the reins and made it conditional. But when we put our trust in God in the midst of the battle, He will strengthen us with His power and love, and the Holy Spirit comforts us as we walk through painful paths.

It helps to know that even Jesus faced the same issue in the Garden of Gethsemane when He asked the Father, *"O My Father, if it is possible, let this cup pass from Me; nevertheless, not as I will, but as You will"* ~ Matthew 26:39. The pressures we endure as we pass through some of the storms in our life can cause us to question whether we can go any further, but like Jesus, we can surrender our will to the Father and allow Him to carry us when we are weak.

The secret to making it through the storm to the other side is to focus on today. Jesus said in the sermon on the mount, *"therefore do not worry about tomorrow, for tomorrow will worry about its own things. Sufficient for the day is its own trouble"* ~ Matthew 6:34.

Our walk with the Lord is a daily journey. Our walking companion is the Holy Spirit. We are encouraged by Paul in Galatians where he says, *"I say then: Walk in the Spirit, and you shall not fulfill the lust of the flesh"* Galatians 5:16. When we are in step with the Holy Spirit, He will keep us from going back to our natural tendencies in the flesh. These can include doubts and temptations to put our trust in our own thoughts and feelings rather than in God. However, the writer of Proverbs tells us, *"Trust in the LORD with all your heart, And lean not on your own understanding; In all your ways acknowledge Him, And He shall direct your paths"* ~ Proverbs 3:5-6.

The most challenging part of that verse to follow is to not lean on our understanding. By default, when we face most of life's problems, we tend to try and solve them from our knowledge and experience, and for many of those issues, that will be perfectly fine. However, for God to direct our paths, all of our decisions should be flexible where we allow space for the Lord to move and make changes, should He choose to do so.

One of the keys to peaceful acceptance, when our prayers are not answered the way we expected, is first to acknowledge that God is ultimately good and that He wants only the best for us. When we have that level of trust in the Lord, we are in a place that is much more able to adapt to the answer the Lord has in mind.

Many times, the direction that God is leading next may seem like a mistake to us. The answer to our prayers may not seem like an answer at all and certainly does not make any sense from our viewpoint of the situation! Remember, though; our God is not limited to our list of options on how to go about fixing things. He always works outside of the box, surprising us with answers we could never have imagined. Sometimes the wisdom of His response may only be seen in retrospect or maybe, not at all, this side of Heaven.

It helps to remember that as opposed to us, God has a complete view of the situation and knows what would be the best course that will fit within His plans and also be eternally beneficial for us. As Isaiah tells us, *"For My thoughts are not your thoughts, nor are your ways My ways,"* says the LORD. *"For as the heavens are higher than the earth, so are My ways higher than your ways, And My thoughts than your thoughts"* ~ Isaiah 55:8-9.

Storm Proofs

- New life in Christ can only grow when we are dead to self.
- When the Father says, *"no,"* it means He's got something better.
- When we surrender our will, we are in a place to receive God's best.

Chapter 6

THE PURPOSE OF THE STORM

"I am the vine; you are the branches. He who abides in Me, and I in him, bears much fruit; for without Me you can do nothing." ~ John 15:5

From the time we became new Christians, God, through the Holy Spirit, has been working to make us into the image of Jesus, as Paul states in Romans 8:29. In 1 Corinthians 3:1-2, Paul describes how we start out as "babes in Christ" fed by the milk of the Word before we can move on to meat, meaning the deeper truths of our faith.

There is a progression of maturity that is expected as we seek to grow in our relationship with God. However, we may often stop at a point where we feel comfortable and are not interested in venturing out any further from the shore. At this point, for God to move us forward in His plan for us, He will often allow us to pass through situations that leave us totally dependent on Him.

An example of this I like is when I think about how we taught our children to walk. They have finally been able to stand up on their own, sometimes balancing on a piece of furniture beside them to steady themselves, and they have that look like, *"I'm going to come to you."* This is usually followed by one or two steps before falling or sitting on the floor. Over time and several tries, they will go on to successfully make it those first few steps to Mom and Dad.

The toddler could have stopped there and just keep repeating those few steps, but Mom and Dad knows that they need to keep challenging their child with new limits so they can walk confidently anywhere. Each time the baby would master a few steps more, Mom and Dad would back up a little further and encourage the baby to come to them.

It's interesting to note that although there may be moments of hesitation, the baby will usually continue to test their limits, especially as they see their parents encouraging them as they try. They don't sit down and reason that they've mastered those first six to ten steps, so why bother wearing themselves out or that Mom or Dad can carry them the rest of the way from then on. That would neither be practical or acceptable in our desire to see them grow. Instead, the toddler just sees their parent on the other side of the room and determine to make it over there.

As adults, we often make the mistake of stopping from going deeper with God when our feet can no longer touch the bottom as we move out. We're not willing to let go of our ability to manage our circumstances if things change, and we want to retreat to a safer depth nearer to shore.

I know that was the case with myself from the time I was very young until even now. I enjoyed going to the beach and swimming, but I didn't like to be out farther than my feet could touch or see the bottom. I was comfortable being in the deep end of a swimming pool. I could see the bottom and was close enough to the edge if I wanted to get out. But swimming at a beach was a different experience. I needed a greater sense of control in that environment.

If left to us, we would often be happy just to keep circling in our small familiar pond, not desiring to go beyond the limits we've become accustomed to. We may look out and view the waters that lead to God's vast ocean, but we have little interest in venturing out into the unknown. We reason that venturing further was for more mature Christians and for those who had a special calling on their lives.

However, fear of the unknown could hinder the unique destiny that

God has planned for each of us. If we are willing to trust Him and let go of the things tying us close to the shore, we will begin to experience the fruits of trusting Him fully. Our Lord needs to stretch our faith by taking us away from where we feel secure and in control of our circumstances. He knows we're never going to grow unless we're willing to let go of the things that give us a false sense of security and to step out where we have to depend on Him completely. This place is unfamiliar and even uncomfortable.

One of the aspects of facing a storm is the element of surprise. Without warning, it moves in upon us quickly and catches us off guard. When our prayers seem to go unanswered, we desperately move into panic mode to control things before becoming worse. Panic is usually prompted by fear, and when fear enters your boat, faith is the first casualty overboard. The two cannot exist side by side. We must choose one or the other.

Another reaction we have when encountering storms within our lives is to ask, *"Why is this happening to me?"* Oftentimes, we'll do a quick spiritual inventory about how faithful we've been and how this situation is not indicative of just how hard we have been working for the Lord. Although the words may not cross our lips, what we're really saying deep down inside is, *"I don't deserve this!"* You may have heard others going through times like this, saying, *"if that's how I'm rewarded, then why do I even bother?"*

If we are not careful, we can easily fall into feeling sorry for ourselves. Our sense of self-righteous indignation can even cause us to question God's goodness toward us, but the truth is just the opposite. When we study the scriptures, we see example after example of heroes of the faith who endured terrible injustices in their walk with God, such as Joseph, David, Esther, and Job, to name a few. But in each case, that was not the end of their story. In the end, Joseph became second in command to Pharaoh of all of Egypt, David became King of Israel, Esther became queen to King Ahasuerus, and Job had twice the amount restored to him than what he had lost.

We need to be discerning as to what the Lord is trying to do when we pass through storms in our life. It's hard to understand the things that are happening around us when standing in the middle of a storm. All we may see when we look out is the chaos surrounding us. We cry out to God to remove the circumstance, but when nothing changes, we start to feel all alone, wondering if the Lord has heard us at all.

Our life's challenges aren't much different from what the disciples felt as they looked out at the wind and waves slowly making its way into the boat. They felt alone and helpless amid the storm. Despite their experience of fishing at night and skills at controlling their boats in difficult situations, this was one of those times they could not prevail over the circumstances against them. These are times when we are not picked up by God or where He calms the storm then gently sets us back down again. Instead, the Lord steps back and stretches our faith, saying, *"do you trust me? Then get out of your boat, keep your eyes on Me and come to Me."*

One of the primary purposes of a storm is to cause us to let go of whatever else we may be holding onto for safety and learn to focus only on Jesus to see us through it. It is a time that checks how deep the roots of our faith go down.

Then there are times when we are caught in the crucible of life where our faith is severely tested. We look around for help to find our way out, and there is no one around to guide us and nothing to hold onto to save us. The situation can be as dark as the night the disciples found themselves in, with little hope as the water filled their boat. When things are going our way, we can say and think that our faith is very strong, but when the storm is rocking our boat, then we can see exactly where the strength of our faith really lies.

There is an overwhelming, all-consuming sense of helplessness, and at that moment, we are standing between the choices of faith or fear; of reaching down and trusting the Lord to either deliver us, bring us through on the other side of the trial or we can give up and allow the storm to sweep us under.

There's another example of this from scripture: After Job had lost all of his wealth and earthly possessions and all of his children had been killed in an accident, Job himself, according to the Bible, was smitten with boils from his head to his feet so that he took a potsherd to scrape himself as he sat amid the ashes.

It's important to note that Job had no knowledge about why he was suffering these tragedies which suddenly came upon him and his family. He had led such a righteous life that this should not be the fate of anyone as devoted to God as Job had been. In the midst of his losses we're told that Job's wife said to him, *"Do you still hold fast to your integrity? Curse God and die!"* ~ Job 2:9. Scripture doesn't tell us anything about Job's wife's faith in God, but her tirade against Job implies anger and bitterness towards God for what has happened. Job, for his part, was not prepared to follow in her footsteps but told her, *"You speak as one of the foolish women speaks. Shall we indeed accept good from God, and shall we not accept adversity?"* ~ Job 2:10. Then the second part of verse 10 goes on to say, *"In all this Job did not sin with his lips."*

Circumstances like this would be enough to cause many to give up on God. The ensuing grief and pain could trigger a whole of range of emotions deep into our soul, such as doubt, disillusionment, frustration, anger, and bitterness, to name a few, locking out any chance of a healthy perspective. On the other hand, Job showed incredible restraint and wisdom in the midst of grief and sorrow that allowed him not to sin by judging God's motives. This kind of response can only come from someone whose strong relationship with God will enable them to trust Him even when the understanding is not there to comfort them.

However, this is the very question that will define our faith and keeps us awake at night, asking, *"Why?"* As human beings, we have an insatiable need to know why things happen the way they do, and then the answer will determine whether we accept it. It has to pass all of our inherent feelings of right and wrong and what's fair or unjust in our eyes. If we fail to decipher the *"whys,"* we also tend to dismiss the Author's explanation.

This heart attitude is why many may walk away disillusioned with God because He did not spare them from the peril of the storm. Instead, they experienced silence and aloneness. The only thing that can secure us is faith. The book of Hebrews says, *"Now faith is the substance of things hoped for, the evidence of things not seen"* ~ Hebrews 11:1. If God sat down and explained everything to us as He was doing it, we would not need faith. But faith is trusting God when there is no understanding of the situation. Like the disciples, we can't see our way in the night, but we still believe God will take us through to the other side. This kind of faith comes from a close relationship with the Lord that is established before we encounter the storms ahead of us.

Storm Proofs

- God allows trials to develop character and a deeper trust in Him so we will let go of everything else and focus on Him only.
- The Bible illustrates how everyone who follows Him encounter storms at some point.
- When the storm has passed, is our faith stronger or weaker?

Chapter 7

A TRIP TO THE POTTER'S HOUSE

"But now, O LORD, You are our Father; We are the clay, and You our potter; and all we are the work of Your hand." ~ Isaiah 64:8

Many years ago, my wife decided to join a friend who was taking classes working with ceramics. Unlike the story we read in Jeremiah 18, where the potter is fashioning a vessel from clay, the ceramics that my wife and her friend worked with were already formed molds.

She would start by selecting the mold she wanted to work with. This was usually an animal, maybe a dog or tiger cub, etc. Then she would proceed to sand it down, apply a glaze to it, and then, when ready, would leave it with the leader for it to be fired in the kiln. This stage of the process was vital in order for the vessel to harden so it could withstand the pressures during use later on. Without this step, the vessel would never realize its potential but remain a piece simply set on a shelf to be looked at.

The Lord says in Proverbs 17:3, *"The refining pot is for silver and the furnace for gold, But the Lord tests the hearts."* To purify gold in ancient times, an artisan would heat the gold in a crucible until it was molten. Then while stirring it, he would skim off the impurities that rose to the surface. The Bible calls the impurities "dross." The dictionary defines dross as a mass of impurities floating on the top of molten metal. This dross had no value and was removed in order to purify the final product of the metal being heated.

After salvation, God sets about to transform us from our sinful nature into the image of Christ. *"For whom He foreknew, He also predestined to be conformed to the image of His Son, that He might be the firstborn among many brethren"* ~ Romans 8:29. An image of that is seen in Jeremiah 18, where the potter takes the clay that had become marred in his hands and remakes it into another vessel. This endless transformation process will go on for the rest of our lives until the Lord takes us home as we can never be perfect this side of heaven. There will be so many steps and lessons to be learned as He gently changes us from one stage to the next.

However, for us to be prepared for use in His future plans for us, there are times when we will need to pass through the trials that James talks about in James 1:2-4, *"My brethren, count it all joy when you fall into various trials, knowing that the testing of your faith produces patience. But let patience have its perfect work, that you may be perfect and complete, lacking nothing."* Whether we like it or not, faith grows through the trials we endure. As scripture portrays, trials are a test of our faith. It does not take faith to make it through the good times.

On our spiritual journey, there will be times where God allows our faith to be tested by fire. The circumstances are often intense as they are meant to stretch our limits to where we see the Lord as the only "lifeboat" that is able to deliver us in the situation. With each trial, God is refining and shaping us more and more into the image of our Saviour. It is part of a lifelong make-over from the inside, the transformation of our hearts.

Our Home Reno

Over the years, my wife and I enjoyed watching some of the programs on television that dealt with home renovations performed by professional contractors instead of DIY. Like the potter who took the marred vessel of clay and made it over into something new, the renovators would go in based upon the plan they knew would improve the home's functionality and overall value.

During the initial process of the reno, they would often have to gut and take out many of the existing walls and handiwork that stood in the way of the planned make-over. These changes would be expected by the owners, who are usually happy to see the demolition. Sometimes, the contractor's expert eye will come across issues that are not as obvious, such as hidden behind walls, under flooring, above the ceiling, and the list goes on. Problems like the electrical being dangerous or out of code, water seepage, etc., invariably are problems that the owners were not aware of and dig deeply into the renovation budget.

These unexpected issues are like our "blind spots". When God begins to uncover those areas in our lives, we may be reluctant to let go and change. We may not have realized that they are the very issues hindering our spiritual growth, but the Holy Spirit has gently been nudging us to deal with them. This could be in the case with relationships, habits, the way we spend our money, or many other things that we never questioned before, but God is asking us now to surrender them and to trust Him.

The renovations have a two-part stage though. As we knock down the walls where God wants to move in, there is now room for the Holy Spirit to begin growing God's character in our lives in the form of the fruit of the Spirit.

God is our Master Builder. He has a plan for our lives that can only be put into action when we are willing to give over the deed of our lives back to Him with full permission to make any changes He deems necessary. The cost of the renovation has already been paid for by the blood of Jesus.

Along with the sins we have been forgiven of, there are things in our lives that God wants to prune and remove after we have been adopted into His family. We need to be aware that from the time we accepted Jesus to be our Saviour, the Holy Spirit then moves into our heart to begin the process of working from the inside. He executes the Father's plan to transform us from who we used to be into the person we were meant to be. Paul sums it up in his letter to the church in Corinth by saying,

"Therefore, if anyone is in Christ, he is a new creation; old things have passed away; behold, all things have become new" ~ 2 Corinthians 5:17.

Our understanding of salvation can sometimes leave us feeling as though we are poor adopted orphans standing timidly just inside the doors of God's Kingdom. It's important that we go on to discover the full knowledge of our inheritance as children of the King. It is when we lay down all of our rags of mistaken self-worth at the foot of the cross that we can then put on the robes of sonship that the Father has been longing to clothe us with because now we are home!

Storm Proofs

- The molding of our faith is strengthened by the fiery trials that we face.
- God is the Master Builder Who transforms us into the image of Jesus.
- The Father loves us too much to leave us as we were.

Chapter 8

THE EYE OF THE STORM

"He who dwells in the secret place of the Most High, shall abide under the shadow of the Almighty" Psalm 91:1

The old testament in Deuteronomy 31:6 and 8 says, vs. 6, *"Be strong and of good courage, do not fear nor be afraid of them; for the LORD your God, He is the One who goes with you. He will not leave you nor forsake you."* Vs. 8, *"And the LORD, He is the One who goes before you. He will be with you. He will not leave you nor forsake you; do not fear nor be dismayed."* Moses was encouraging Joshua, who was to lead Israel into the promised land after his death. Moses told Joshua twice that the Lord would never leave or forsake him. This promise is also stated again in Hebrews 13:5 of the New Testament.

Although we may feel alone when the storm is pressing in, and the future looks dark, the truth is, God has never left us and will not forsake us. Like Joshua, He calls on us to be strong and courageous, to exercise our spiritual muscles, and trust Him to deliver us from our circumstances. That could mean either calming the storm or protecting and keeping us as we go through it with Him.

The important thing to remember is that Jesus is with us in the midst of it. The disciples were not alone or forgotten even though when they left, Jesus had stayed back to spend time in prayer. Jesus still had His eye on the boat and was aware of their dilemma as they tried to overcome the elements.

When our faith is being stretched and tested, Jesus knows just the right time to come alongside to help us. It's usually after we realize we cannot turn the situation around by ourselves, then we begin to shift our focus to God alone to rescue us from peril. This often means that we are in a place where we have run out of options, and we are desperate to grab onto anything that will support us in our time of need. Sometimes, it feels as though the floor beneath us is giving out and there's no one else who can help us. Our focus now changes, and we begin look intensely to Jesus to come and do what only He can do. When our boat is taking on water, and we realize it's no longer our source of safety, the Lord has brought us to a place where we become totally dependent on Him.

Peace won't always arrive immediately in the midst of the circumstances as it did when Jesus stood up and rebuked the wind and the waves, but rather, it abides in us wherever we are, when we live a life that is centered on Him. This is the answer to living in the eye of the storm.

Hurricanes move in with a tremendous and devastating force that packs a double punch. People will be warned in advance to prepare by either boarding up and laying low until it has passed over or to board up and leave for a safer location as far away as possible. After enduring the first assault of the hurricane, the winds will slowly fade as the eye of the storm passes over the path of a direct hit. The weather will seem relatively clear for a short period before the second half of the hurricane passes over.

The thing that stands out most about the eye of the storm is that it remains calm, but only for a brief period, while chaos and destruction are still raining down upon everything surrounding it. The circumstances have not changed. As we look around us, the problems of the storm are still there. We may say to ourselves, *"Why can't we just stay in the eye where it's safe, and the storm can't touch us?"* However, Jesus never said that we would be exempt from trouble but just the opposite. He said, *"These things I have spoken to you, that in Me you may have peace. In the world you will have tribulation; but be of good cheer, I have overcome the world"* ~ John 16:33. In this passage, Jesus affirms that as long as we live in our fallen world, we will have the same troubles that everyone else is subject to. But even though we will encounter trials, He encourages us that we can find peace in Him in spite of them.

Therefore, we don't need to try and search for an "eye" to our storm whenever they hit because Jesus is the "eye" that sees us through to the other side! If we are in Christ and Jesus abides in us, then His peace abides in us also. His love and the Holy Spirit, from Whom we can draw comfort, are always with us as we allow Jesus to navigate the path through the storm.

An example of God's peace in dire situations is found in the Old Testament's story of Shadrach, Meshach, and Abednego, three young Jewish men who were taken as slaves along with Daniel during Israel's exile to Babylon.

In the story, King Nebuchadnezzar had a statue made that was ninety feet high and nine feet wide. The people were instructed that when the music begins to play, everyone must bow down and worship the image the king had set up. Anyone who did not immediately do so was to be thrown into a blazing furnace. However, this was not an option for Shadrach, Meshach, and Abednego as they would only worship the God of Israel.

When the king was told of their disobedience to his command, he had them brought before him and gave them one more chance to comply, saying, *"And who is the god who will deliver you from my hands?"* Daniel 3:15b, but the three answered, *"O Nebuchadnezzar, we have no need to answer you in this matter. If that is the case, our God whom we serve is able to deliver us from the burning fiery furnace, and He will deliver us from your hand, O king. But if not, let it be known to you, O king, that we do not serve your gods, nor will we worship the gold image which you have set up"* ~ Daniel 3:16-18.

The courage of these three young men is captured in the words, *"but if not."* At the time, they had no way of knowing how things would turn out. They were in a desperate place and were willing to place their lives in the hands of the God of Israel, no matter what the outcome.

The rest of the story goes on to tell how they were tossed into the furnace that had been ordered to be heated seven times hotter than before so that even the soldiers who bound them and escorted Shadrach, Meshach, and Abednego to the furnace were burned up before they could put them in.

Soon after, King Nebuchadnezzar looked at the blazing inferno and said, *"did we not cast three men bound into the midst of the fire?"* They answered and said to the king, *"True, O king."* *"Look!"* he answered, *"I see four men loose, walking in the midst of the fire; and they are not hurt, and the form of the fourth is like the Son of God"* ~ Daniel 3:24b-25.

When the king commanded that the three Hebrew boys be brought out from the furnace, he noticed that their hair and clothes were not burned, neither did they even have the smell of smoke on them! The God of Israel had saved them! After this profound miracle, Shadrach, Meshach, and Abednego were promoted in the province of Babylon with the edict that anyone who spoke anything against their God would be killed and their houses reduced to ashes because there was no other God that could deliver like this!

This brings up another point regarding the storms we weather in our lives. Whether we realize it or not, our testimony is on display for all to see as we handle our problems. In the case of Shadrach, Meshach, and Abednego, their faithfulness and God's deliverance impacted King Nebuchadnezzar, causing him to exalt the God of Israel in Babylon and promote those three men in his kingdom.

The above story is intended to strengthen our faith in the God Who can deliver. It does not mean that we should grit our teeth and be unnatural in our response to the trials we are facing or pretend that we have everything under control when we are clearly devastated by the circumstances we are going through. People need to see the struggles we are facing to be able to relate to how we respond in an honest manner.

The way we respond in the case of a tragedy becomes very apparent where there are endless questions and seemingly no answers that will satisfy the inevitable question of *"Why?"* It's important to know that, even as a Christian, we are never called upon to have all of the answers or feel the need to explain situations that defy all reason. Sometimes, we may simply need to leave them at the feet of Jesus and trust that He will see us through as long as we are anchored in Him.

When the answer we were seeking to our prayers does not arrive, and we feel swept away by the undertow of ensuing grief, the thought may cross our minds that we are not displaying Christ in the right way to unbelievers or maybe, even believers. But this is not the truth. God made us in His image with emotions that can be overwhelmed and shattered like anyone else. We may experience times of anger and frustration, discouragement, and even disillusionment as we pass through a range of reactions in coping with the loss we have suffered.

The only question that needs to be asked in such cases is, *"Have we lost our hope?"* This will be the ultimate factor that others will notice in our response to tragedy. Did we blame God and throw in the towel, or did we continue to trust Him to lead us out of this dark time?

David encouraged us when he wrote, *"yea, though I walk through the valley of the shadow of death, I will fear no evil; For You are with me"* ~ Psalm 23:4. The key here is not that David didn't experience these things but that he took comfort from the fact that he did not walk that path alone because God was with him.

Understanding, in such events, as we have noted before, is a luxury we may not be given this side of heaven, but our steadfast faith in God, in the midst of everything else we may be feeling, will speak to those around us that our hope in Him has not changed.

Storm Proofs

- Jesus wants us to be totally dependent on Him.
- Jesus is the "Eye" of the storm.
- He is the Prince of Peace living inside of us by the Holy Spirit.
- Are you living a life of *"Even if?"*

Chapter 9

AN "OUT OF THE BOAT" EXPERIENCE

"And Peter answered Him and said, 'Lord, if it is You, command me to come to You on the water.'" So He said, "Come." ~ Matthew 14:28-29a

Somewhere around 2010, my wife became involved with ministering at a mission in downtown Toronto under the leadership of a pastor and friend from our church who was mentoring her at this mission on Monday nights. The area was quite rough and was inhabited by many who were homeless and those with addictions. It was a simple setting where people would wander in off the street and sit down to listen as they shared the gospel and maybe enjoy some light refreshments.

The pastor asked if I would join them and come down from work maybe twice a month to share a word from the Lord. Kim had already asked me if I would do that, but I had declined at first, saying the commute was too long from where I worked, and it would be very late by the time we would arrive back home with work the next day. However, when the pastor asked if I would consider a couple of times a month, I agreed to try it and would see how things went.

From the first night I went, I felt such compassion for the people who were coming to hear the Good News shared in an informal atmosphere. It was clear that many of them may not have owned much more than the clothes they were wearing and were very grateful for the few things we could offer them, such as coffee and sometimes a slice of pizza. I knew from that point that I wanted to become involved and come down each week that I could after that.

After doing that for a few years, we felt the calling to start a separate ministry of our own. The mission was run by someone else who opened it up to various Christian groups to use on different days and times of the week, but we were sensing the Lord, leading us to start an independent outreach somewhere in the area. The people's needs were obviously not only in material things but also in hearing the Word of God's unconditional love.

In 2013, Kim and I were ordained by an independent Christian ministry interested in raising pastors that would start their own ministry and allow them to fulfill the call and giftings the Lord had given them.

We started out modestly in 2014 after church on Sundays, holding meetings in the upstairs community room of the public library close to St. James Town. I said that these meetings were practice sessions for preaching since the only ones to attend were the leaders, and sometimes some friends would join us. However, with some advertising around the neighborhood, we successfully held a back-to-school event at the end of summer and a large Christmas party for kids and families that year that was both very successful.

In 2015, we obtained an agreement with a bakery close to where we lived to donate their surplus baked goods to us weekly. We would pick them up on Friday evenings and take them downtown on Saturday afternoons to a park area a few blocks away from where the library was to give out to the residents in the area.

In 2016, my wife and I felt led by the Lord to leave our church and join with some other leaders who had a vision to start an outreach in St. James Town, an impoverished area in downtown Toronto. At the time, the leadership of our church prayed for us the last Sunday we were there, but I don't think there was a clear understanding of what we were going to do or why we had to leave. I explained that I felt compelled by the Lord to reach out and share the love of God with these people.

We worked as an independent, non-denominational ministry that was not endorsed or supported financially by any church or institution. I often referred to our work there as a labour of love because the level of poverty meant that all of our overhead expenses would have to be borne by the leaders themselves.

In March of 2016, on Sundays, we started renting the smaller of two gymnasiums at the public school right next to the park where we gave out the food each Saturday. This gave us the opportunity to share the gospel for a couple of hours. We were eager to do this on Saturdays but did not have the time when giving out the food in order to keep the line moving. The weekly services lasted through the end of 2016, but then when some of the leaders moved on to other things, our finances dropped, and we couldn't afford to rent the gymnasium anymore on a weekly basis.

Over the few years we have been there so far, the outreach has grown to include large events such as community barbeques, a Thanksgiving dinner, Christmas parties that saw the gospel shared, meals enjoyed, gifts given out, and clothing distributed to those in need.

Although God has been faithful in providing all of the resources to minister to the people there, it has definitely been an "out of boat" experience, where "walking on water" meant letting go of all of the typical people and places we would rely on for support to reach those in St. James Town. We simply had to walk by faith in the vision the Lord had laid upon our hearts and pray that God would show up strong in our weaknesses, and He has never failed to do so!

Storm Proofs

- When God calls you to *"Get out of your boat"* it is a walk by faith not by sight experience.
- Walking on water begins with obedience.

Chapter 10

WHAT IS YOUR BOAT MADE OF?

"For no other foundation can anyone lay than that which is laid, which is Jesus Christ" ~ 1 Corinthians 3:11

When examining what our boat is made of, the question is really about our faith. What have we ultimately put our trust in for our lives? Whether by conscious or unconscious choice, the place of our trust is often exposed when we find ourselves in situations of extreme pressure. When our relationship with God is put to the test, it will show how deep and sincere our faith really is. When the pressures of life squeeze us on all sides, whatever is inside us, will ultimately come out.

If we need evidence of how incomparably important our relationship with God is, we only need to look to the cross. Here at the cross, we see how far Jesus went to remove the wall of sin which stood blocking access to the Father. Once we have accepted Jesus into our hearts as our Saviour, He jumps on board with full-fledged commitment in building and strengthening our relationship with Him. He works to transform us into the person we were intended to be.

There's an expression that goes, *"Jesus is Lord of all, or He's not Lord at all."* This means that the Lord comes first, above everything else. Anything else would be an idol. An idol is simply someone or something else taking the rightful place of God in our lives.

Our Identity

Our identity is rooted in who has first place in our lives. So how would you describe your identity? What would you say defines you? As Christians, we would probably share statements about our faith in Jesus Christ as being the essence of our identity, which is good. But is that really all that others would say when they examine our lives in the public arena?

For many, identity can be closely related to social standing, marital status, or being part of an elite group. Though a good job, academic success, or financial stability are honourable accomplishments, these things can become part of our identity. Even as Christians, we may find our identity in such things as what church we attend, the denomination we belong to, the calling on our lives, giftings we've received, our position, or our function within the church. This attitude can sometimes be seen in a believer who tells everyone what spiritual gifts they are operating in. But what are they really saying, and what does it say about them?

In a performance-based world, it may be challenging to separate our identity from our achievements or those things that we can control. There's this inner propensity to think that we could somehow play a part in earning our identity in Christ.

All of those things mentioned above are merely an attempt to find purpose or significance from something other than the simple fact that we are one of God's children. God has designed us for relationship with Him. So, it's not surprising when non-Christians try to find their identity or define themselves by worldly substitutes for God. It's part of humanity's on-going search to find meaning and purpose for their lives outside of the revelation of God's grace revealed in Jesus Christ.

At the very heart of the gospel is the message of grace. The Father freely offered us grace as a gift in the person of Jesus. A gift cannot be earned, or it is no longer a gift but a reward. Paul said it this way in Ephesians 2: 8-9, *"For by grace you have been saved through faith, and that not of yourselves; it is the gift of God, not of works, lest anyone should boast."*

Even as Christians, there are times without realizing it, we may put our faith or sense of security in the same things the world does and not totally upon the Lord Jesus Christ and His finished work on the cross. When our identity relies on anything else but Jesus, our foundation is unstable, as Jesus described in Matthew 7:24-27. In this parable, Jesus taught that if one's "house" is built upon sand (things), that house shall crumble when put to the test in the storms of life.

There are two stories in the Bible that will help to illustrate the choice we need to make to ensure we are placing our faith in Christ alone. The first one is about the rich young ruler in Luke 18. The second one is Zacchaeus, the tax collector in Luke 19.

In Luke 18, the rich young ruler wanted to know what he must "do" to have eternal life. Like most people, he expects that eternal life or salvation can be earned by doing specific things or acting in a certain way that portrays a holy lifestyle. So, Jesus gives him an answer based upon the requirements of the law. However, the commandments that Jesus quoted were those commandments (vs. 6 to 9) that related to our treatment of one another.

The rich young ruler feels rather comfortable and confident saying that he has kept those commandments from his youth up, in essence, earning any favour that God would show him. At this point, Mark records that Jesus looked at him and *loved him*.

When the young ruler asked what he still lacked, Jesus replied, *"Go sell what you have and give to the poor then come and follow Me."* If the rich young ruler was trying to obtain eternal life by keeping the commandments, Jesus exposed the area in which he was not obeying God, and that was the first commandment, *"You shall have no other gods before Me"* ~ Exodus 20:3.

Jesus recognized the desire in the young ruler's heart to draw closer to God, but he also knew that his riches were taking God's place in his heart. When he challenged him to sell and give to the poor, the rich young ruler became very sad and chose his riches over eternal life. He was not willing to let go of his wealth to follow Jesus.

To this, Jesus says in Matthew 6:24, *"no one can serve two masters; for either he will hate the one and love the other, or else he will be loyal to the one and despise the other. You cannot serve God and mammon."* Anything that we are holding onto that prevents us from putting God first is indeed our God and idol. Jesus cannot be the Lord of our lives if another is sitting upon the throne of our hearts.

Jesus said, *"Then He said to them all, 'If anyone desires to come after Me, let him deny himself, and take up his cross daily, and follow Me. For whoever desires to save his life will lose it, but whoever loses his life for My sake will save it. For what profit is it to a man if he gains the whole world, and is himself destroyed or lost?'"* ~ Luke 9:23-25.

When we follow Jesus, we are dead to "self". That's what "taking up our cross" means. It's a place of sacrifice and total surrender in order to be truly alive in Christ. Like a marriage, it is a solemn covenant between you and God, forsaking everyone and everything else to put Him first. The rich young ruler was not prepared to make that commitment but instead walked away from Jesus.

In Luke 19, we read the story about a man named Zacchaeus, a chief tax collector for the Romans. The Romans used the Jews to collect their taxes for them. Matthew, one of Jesus' disciples, is another example of a tax collector in the New Testament. However, collecting taxes for the Romans from their fellow countrymen would usually mean that people like Zacchaeus and Matthew were looked upon as traitors and sinners. They were despised by their fellow Jews and treated as outcasts. They were often rich, as much of it came from overcharging for taxes owed and pocketing the difference.

From the little we read about Zacchaeus in the scriptures, I sensed that Zacchaeus was a lonely man. Due to his line of work, the only friends he may have had were other tax collectors. His fellow Jews hated him, and the Romans were only using him. Although he had more than enough money, it could not replace his longing for love and acceptance.

But today is different. Scripture says that Zacchaeus wanted to see Jesus as He passed on His way through Jericho, but being a short man, he could not see Him over the crowd. Therefore, he decided to run ahead and climb a sycamore tree to get a better view of Jesus as He passed by. In a way, it's a picture of how he must have seen himself within the community; alone, sitting on the outside looking in but not welcomed to join with the crowd as they followed Jesus.

Then, something unthinkable happened; something that would change Zacchaeus forever. Jesus doesn't merely take notice of Zacchaeus sitting in the tree but instead, stopped and said to him, *"Zacchaeus, make haste and come down, for today I must stay at your house"* ~ Luke 19:5. I'm surprised Zacchaeus didn't fall out of the tree from shock! Instead, he came down quickly and welcomed Jesus into his house.

This act does not go unnoticed by the people there. Like so many other times when Jesus took time out to fellowship with people who were thought to be unworthy of His attention, those around began to question why Jesus would bother with a man like Zacchaeus. It would undoubtedly be more suitable that someone with Jesus' popularity, ministry, and teachings about the Kingdom of God would be better suited to dine with the social elite of His day; the Pharisees, Rabbis, and the "good" people. Instead, Jesus' reputation was reinforced as mentioned in Luke 7:34, *"a friend of tax collectors and sinners."*

This behavior would perplex the pious leadership of Jewish society. However, Jesus would counter their whisperings by saying, *"the Son of Man has come to seek and to save that which was lost"* ~ Luke 19:10.

On the other hand, Zacchaeus was overwhelmed with excitement. Jesus knew who he was and yet cared enough about him as to ignore the social norms of acceptance and actually dine together with him as friends. This act of love from Jesus touched Zacchaeus deeply. He immediately became convicted that being wealthy could not meet the need in his life for peace and fulfillment, especially when it had come by dishonest means.

Zacchaeus began to have a change of heart by being in the presence of Jesus, and he wanted to make things right. He told Jesus that he would donate half of his possessions to the poor and confessed that he would restore it fourfold if he had cheated anyone of their resources. His actions showed that his heart's desire for riches had changed, and he now embraced Jesus and His teachings.

Jesus responded to Zacchaeus, *"Today salvation has come to this house"* ~ Luke 19:9. Jesus knew that a man could not serve both God and money. We see this in the previous chapter of Luke 18 when He encountered the rich young ruler who seemed willing to fulfill all of God's commandments but yet was unwilling to give all his possessions to the poor and follow Jesus. Jesus later said it was easier for a camel to pass through the eye of a needle than for a rich man to enter the kingdom of God.

"Today" was the day of salvation for Zacchaeus as he settled the matter in his heart by choosing to give his wealth over to God's purposes and follow Jesus. I'm sure at that moment he never felt taller in his life! Zacchaeus found the answer to all his longings in the person of Jesus and by letting go of all those things he had tried to fill it with before.

When people do not know Jesus as Lord and Saviour, there's a natural urge to fill the empty places in our hearts with temporary things. We might try to fill that spiritual longing by even following a religion. The act of complying with the various rules and requirements of that discipline as well as performing many good works can give us a certain ease of conscience. But once again, this is a false peace since it results from trying to earn our salvation somehow.

Religion is experiencing God at arm's length. It's long on form and ritual but often leaves no place for the Spirit of God to operate or even be in the Sunday services sometimes. It allows God into our life as a guest but reminds Him that we are still the master of our house. Righteousness is often linked to church attendance, whether we were baptized as a baby, financial donations, good works, charitable endeavors, etc. We can do all of these 'good' things and never know God. Religion is a poor substitute for relationships. Only Jesus Christ can fill the emptiness in our hearts.

Then there are other things that the world may trust in to fill their emptiness, such as drugs, alcohol, worldly relationships, etc., but anything that we place our trust in aside from Jesus Christ and His finished work will never give us the lasting peace and fulfillment we are searching for. At some point, our "boats" will start taking in water, and our safety will be in jeopardy!

The reason I said that people might even trust in other things unconsciously is, even as Christians, we may place our sense of security in the worldly things around us, not intentionally, but simply because we are still living in a world that can affect the way we approach life's situations.

In reference to the case I spoke about in the Foreword of this book regarding my lack of funds and search for work, the Lord showed me through the story of Jesus walking on the water that my boat was sinking because I was trusting in the financial package I received to keep myself and my family safe until I found a new job.

When I finally realized my mistake and repented, I asked the Lord to forgive me. Now my trust and only security would be in Him. After I told my wife about it, although I didn't know what the future held for us, I now had a peace that somehow God would work out everything for our good. About a week later, I started a new job that I was sure the Lord had prepared for me. Lesson learned!

Storm Proofs

- Our true identity is defined by God alone in His Word.
- Religion is a poor substitute for relationship.
- If we put our trust in anything other than Jesus, our boat begins to sink.

Chapter 11

WALKING ON WATER

He who dwells in the secret place of the Most High
Shall abide under the shadow of the Almighty.
I will say of the LORD, "He is my refuge and my fortress;
My God, in Him I will trust."
Surely He shall deliver you from the snare of the fowler
And from the perilous pestilence.
He shall cover you with His feathers,
And under His wings you shall take refuge;
His truth shall be your shield and buckler.
You shall not be afraid of the terror by night,
Nor of the arrow that flies by day,
Nor of the pestilence that walks in darkness,
Nor of the destruction that lays waste at noonday.
A thousand may fall at your side,
And ten thousand at your right hand;
But it shall not come near you.
Only with your eyes shall you look,
And see the reward of the wicked.
Because you have made the LORD, who is my refuge,
Even the Most High, your dwelling place,
No evil shall befall you,
Nor shall any plague come near your dwelling;
For He shall give His angels charge over you,
To keep you in all your ways.
In their hands they shall bear you up,

Lest you dash your foot against a stone.
You shall tread upon the lion and the cobra,
The young lion and the serpent you shall trample underfoot.
"Because he has set his love upon Me, therefore I will deliver him;
I will set him on high, because he has known My name.
He shall call upon Me, and I will answer him;
I will be with him in trouble;
I will deliver him and honor him.
With long life I will satisfy him,
And show him My salvation."
~ Psalm 91

"The victory is won in prayer on the mountain top before the storm, not in the midst of the storm." ~ Gary Byford

Walking on water, symbolically, is simply having a relationship with God that is strong enough and deep enough that we can trust Him no matter what comes against us or what the outcome is. In that place of trust, we know that we can walk through the trials we face, leaning on the Lord for strength and allowing Him to guide us to the other side without being swept under.

In the story of Jesus walking on water, it's important to recognize the time He spent in prayer with His heavenly Father before He left to join the disciples. This is the place we need to find ourselves before we step out to confront the storms that lie ahead.

Each of us would like to enjoy a peaceful life where storms and trials only happen to those who have chosen not to serve God, and if we did encounter such adversity, then Jesus would just step in and calm the wind and waves that were coming against us. However, we know that life doesn't work that way.

Living for Jesus doesn't mean that we get to live inside some kind of protective spiritual bubble where the negative things of life cannot reach us. Instead, sometimes we may think that we have even more troubles after we start to follow the Lord because we are now in opposition to the world around us!

We can begin to feel like the proverbial salmon swimming upstream, but to get where it is seeking to go, it must face the strong current of water rushing downhill in the opposite direction. The fish labors and leaps, making slow progress in its journey to the calmer waters that await at the top, all the while hoping not to encounter any hungry mammals who are looking for an easy meal. So how can we prepare ourselves to meet those challenges when they do occur?

Quiet times are precisely the moments when we should be spending more time in prayer, drawing closer to God, and seeking intimacy with Him. As the passage above encourages us, *"He who dwells in the secret place of the Most High shall abide under the shadow of the Almighty. I will say of the LORD, He is my refuge and my fortress; My God, in Him I will trust"* ~ Psalm 91:1-2.

The above verse speaks of a person who continually trusts and abides in the Lord's presence. In doing so, they recognize that God is the One who gives them sanctuary and protection from their enemies. There is rest and peace in that "secret place" as we are in close communion with our heavenly Father. His shadow covers us as we take refuge under His wings. Psalm 121 expresses the Lord's deep love for His children in the way He watches over and keeps us. Psalm 23, probably the best known of the Psalms, is David's testament to the Lord's intimate care for us as a Shepherd for His sheep.

For those who draw close to the Lord in this way, the scriptures tell us, *"But those who wait on the LORD Shall renew their strength; They shall mount up with wings like eagles, They shall run and not be weary, They shall walk and not faint"* ~ Isaiah 40:31. At those times, the Lord restores our souls and strengthens us for the challenges ahead.

Imagine that you were one of the disciples in the boat that is taking on water and in peril of sinking. What would you do at that point? This adverse situation is a place where the Lord is perfecting our faith and trust in Him. We are, at that moment, given a choice as to how we will react to the situation we are in. I've imagined it before, and except for Peter, I don't think I would have been much different than the other disciples at that time. I would be looking for Jesus and think the conversation would have been something like the following:

"As we wait, numb with uncertainty and desperate to know where Jesus is, we see Him. He was not in the boat but in the distance, walking on the water coming towards us. We call out to Him, and He admonishes us not to be afraid. Then He stops and says to us, 'Get out of the boat.' But we can't get out of the boat? This is where we are safe and protected from the storm. 'You need to get in and help us to overcome this situation just like you have so many times in the past.' 'All this time, you have placed your faith in the boat to take you safely where you were going. You only called on Me when you were in trouble and could not handle it by yourself,' Jesus tells us. 'The boat cannot save you nor protect you from the storm. You must get out of the boat and come to me.'"

Sometimes, God will answer our prayers or meet our needs in a completely different way than how we had imagined He would. From time to time, He may call us to step out of our comfort zone by faith in obedience to Him so that He can offer us something better. The question is, do we trust Him enough to follow? After all, it's easy for us to put our faith in things that we can see and touch, especially when they've formed a pattern in our lives that we've become familiar with.

Right now, Jesus stands waiting as He bids us come. Our response to the request may be similar to Peter's and may make no sense in the natural. But we simply obey because the Master, Jesus bids us, *"come."*

Jesus is always doing the unexpected, and the Father delights in surprising us with how He meets our needs. The key is always to keep our eyes on Jesus. He will sustain us as we step out in faith. But even though we step out in faith, we will inevitably be tempted by distractions. The moment we take our attention off Jesus and focus on the circumstances surrounding us, we may encounter doubts that will draw us down to a place of disillusionment and despair.

It's imperative that we remember the lesson of Peter. At such times, all we need to do is call out to Jesus. He is always there to lift us up and restore us in our walk with Him. He applauds our faith and encourages us to seek His face as we continue to follow Him.

The storm will not last forever. As dark as the skies may seem now, the dawn will surely break again come morning. The sea will be calm again, and our boat afloat and waiting. However, at those times, do we see ourselves still inside the boat, limp with exhaustion from trying to ride out the storm all night by ourselves or resting in the arms of Jesus as we stand with Him upon the water?

Storm Proofs

- Victories are won before our battles, no matter the outcome, when we abide in Jesus.
- Calm times in our life are when we should be drawing closer to God through the Word and prayer.
- Our peace and security is not in our boat but in Jesus alone.

About The Author

Gary Byford is an ordained evangelical minister with Canadian Christian Ministries since 2013 and works with Freedom City Ministries, an independent outreach, serving in St. James Town in downtown Toronto. Along with the other leadership, Gary performs some of the Pastoral Care functions as well as teaching and preaching on occasion.

Born in Montreal, Quebec, Gary has lived in Toronto since 1995 with his wife and family. After 40 years of marriage, his wife Kim went to be with the Lord in 2019 after suffering complications following a heart attack. Gary has two children, Allison and John, and two grandchildren, with whom he enjoys spending much of his time.

After retiring from his secular job in Accounting in late 2019, Gary now spends most of his time pastoring downtown and writing.

Contact Gary:

Email: gmbyford@rogers.com

Gary Byford